Dedication

This book is dedicated to all the Americans who have been denied financing for a home loan, or did not apply for a loan because their credit score was low and they did not think their score was high enough to meet the bank's criteria. In this book you will find programs, investors, or lenders that will lend based upon a buyer's ability to repay, not a FICO score, which does not tell the entire story of a potential buyer. If you follow the instructions in this book you will fulfill your dream of homeownership, save thousands of dollars a year, and build your net worth with a proven blueprint used by investors across the country.

Disclaimer

This book is presented to be available to those who may need accurate information on the subjects covered within. Even though the information has been carefully researched from the best available sources, the author and publisher cannot, and do not, guarantee the accuracy of the information and/or suggestions provided and set forth herein due to the constant changing of programs. The author and/or publisher disclaims any liability for loss, risk, damage, or inconvenience (real or imagined) that may be incurred by, or resulting from, the use of any ideas, information, data, suggestions, opinions, or advice contained in this book. The author and/or publisher do not perform credit repair services. Before utilizing any information in this guide, it is recommended that the services of a competent professional be sought.

Referrals for those services can also be obtained by contacting Financialsecretsrevealed.com or Signature Investments & Consulting Inc.

Scriptures are taken from the King James Version of the Bible.

100 Percent financing for your new home guaranteed. No FICO score requirement!

Sponsors

Editor: Nicole Wagner

Typesetting: ELS

Cover Design: S.I.C.

Published by Signature Investments & Consulting Inc.

Email: Signatureinvestments14@gmail.com

P.O. Box 454, Maywood, Illinois 60153

ISBN: 978-0-9716179-1-9

Library of Congress: 1-4015436171

Printed in the United States of America

Acknowledgments

I thank and praise God for the grace to write another book. I acknowledge my children Prince Neko & Brianna Strong, friends, and fans that motivate me to share principles to building financial freedom.

I give a special acknowledgement to my grandfather, the Honorable Reverend Isaac Strong Sr., my grandmother Rosa Strong, and my mother Deborah James for teaching me sound Christian principles at a young age. I also thank God for spiritual leaders whom I had the pleasure to learn from over the years, like Bishop O.C. Booker of Tabernacle Church of God in Christ, Apostle Donald L. Alford of Progressive Life Giving Word, and Pastor Rob Thompson of Family Harvest Church, to name a few.

About the Writer

I started my real estate career as a loan officer, which gave me an edge because I knew exactly what the banks wanted and required to fund a deal.

I was fortunate enough to service experienced investors as a loan officer. The investors that taught me how to buy and sell were making millions of dollars every year.

During the twenty years that I have been in real estate I've gained priceless information in the following areas, and I specialize in teaching my clients proven financial secrets to retire and build wealth for their future.

Foreclosures	FHA Loans
Short Sales	VA Loans
REO's	Government Vouchers
Property Management	Section 8 Vouchers
Creative Financing	Tax Sales
New Construction	Assuming a Mortgage
Building & Developing	Corporate Credit
Land Contracts	Business Credit
Wholesaling	Investment Properties

Real Estate Auctions	Acquiring Free Land
Building Retirement	Non Performing Notes
Commercial Real Estate	Flipping Homes

I also share a burning desire to educate and share principles of wealth with people looking to grow, learn, and fulfill their goals in life. As a writer, I'm committed to sharing the knowledge and blueprints I've attained to service the middle class and poor.

Table of Contents

Chapter 1.

<u>Importance of Home Ownership</u>

Homeownership is one of the largest investments that most Americans will ever purchase in their life. Americans that own homes enjoy the space and comfort of owning a home and most importantly, their mortgage payment goes toward the principal and interest of the balance owed on the home.

Whether you're purchasing a home for your kids or buying a home because you're tired of paying rent, purchasing a home is a wise decision. As you may already know, if you're paying rent, you're assisting the landlord or owner of the building in paying off his/her mortgage. If the owner of the house or apartment building where you rent owns the building free and clear from the bank, the rent that you pay the landlord is income minus the taxes and insurance paid for the property.

So, in a lot of cases renters are paying for the landlord's building or making the landlord rich. Why not pay yourself? Or, pay into your future by owning a home and allowing your old rent to become a mortgage payment for your home.

In addition to paying into your future, you have several options that you can exercise that place you in an excellent financial position.

Imagine buying a home for $300,000 between the age of 25-30 years old. You take out a traditional conventional mortgage for thirty years. In the next thirty years of your life, you would own your home free and clear. If the area where you purchased the home maintained the value or increased in value over the thirty year period you would have $300,000 in equity.

The equity can be used to secure a line of credit to start a business, which is a common practice for most American business owners. You could also take out a home equity loan to pay your children's or grandchildren's college tuition. Also, as a homeowner you can take out $100,000 to place in an investment program, a retirement account, or even toward purchasing and apartment building to increase your income from tenants paying rent.

Owned real estate gives you a secure asset to use as collateral when applying for a loan. When banks underwrite loans or review an application for a loan, the banks love to see assets, especially if the asset is paid in full with a zero balance.

Homeownership makes applying for any other loan easier when applicants own assets. In the event that you default on the loan, the bank will have collateral, recourse, or security to pursue a delinquent loan which makes lenders more comfortable to lend.

Chapter 2.

<u>100 Percent Financing by Definition</u>

A lot of people are under the impression that 100 percent financing means that you will not have to bring any money to the closing when you purchase a home. When buying a home, you do have to consider closing cost, which consists of title charges from the title company, homeowner insurance, appraisal, pre-paid interest until your first mortgage payment, and other fees associated with buying a home. When a lender offers you 100 percent financing, they will finance 100 percent of the purchase price, meaning no down payment. **However, you are responsible for your closing cost.**

Depending on where you purchase the home, closing cost typically ranges on average between four and ten thousand dollars when buying a one- to four-unit building. Some lenders will even finance some of your closing cost.

However, the easiest way to have your closing cost paid off is to simply ask the seller to pay it. A lot of buyers negotiate the purchase price, which is always a good strategy, in order to lower the price of a new home. And, most sellers are more than willing to give you a $10,000 discount on a home if you can close in a timely manner.

Experienced buyers have another option. Instead of asking for a $10,000 discount on the purchase price of a home they can simply show the seller their pre-approval from the lender. Then, they tell the seller they can close this deal in 30-45 days if the seller is willing to pay all closing costs.

This method would save the seller from paying another mortgage payment and interest. It would also assist in taking his/her property off the market and having property sold, as opposed to being on the market for possibly another three to six months or longer. Most sellers will agree with you and will gladly pay your closing cost if they know that you are approved for the loan. However, it is important to have all of your required documents submitted to the lender to insure that you will close in a timely manner.

When your loan officer asks you for financial documents such as tax returns, pay stubs, and bank statements, make sure you give the loan officer exactly what he/she asks for the next day. This will keep your file up to date and ready to be submitted to an underwriter for final approval or a loan commitment.

Being prepared and saving your money for closing cost is by far the best solution when buying a home. If the seller is not willing to pay your closing cost, some lenders allow for gifts from immediate family, another loan from credit cards, or secured loans as long as your debt-to-income is within the bank's guidelines.

Chapter 3.

Traditional Financing

If you have a purchased a home before, you are familiar with traditional financing from banks and the requirements and programs they offer. For the benefit of first-time homebuyers I will expound briefly on traditional loans offered from banks.

When purchasing a home through standard banks and mortgage companies, the banks generally offer three types of mortgage loans for homebuyers. The three types of loans are conventional loans, FHA loans, and VA loans.

Conventional mortgages require tier one credit or "A plus" credit to get approved for a mortgage. A conventional loan is a loan that is not insured by any governmental agency. The debt-to-income ratio (ratio of monthly income earned minus the amount of bills you have on your credit report) is typically 28/36 of monthly income. This means, the new proposed mortgage cannot exceed 28 percent of your monthly income, and any other bills that show on your credit report cannot exceed 36 percent of your monthly income. The ratio can vary from bank to bank. Some conventional lenders have been known to go up to fifty percent debt-to-income. However, with most conventional mortgages, even though you may have good credit or a high credit score, a conventional mortgage will still require five to twenty percent down payment. Also, if a borrower's down payment is less than twenty percent, you will be required to have mortgage insurance.

An FHA mortgage is a mortgage issued by federally-approved lenders and insured by the Federal Housing Administration (FHA). FHA loans were created for low-to moderate income borrowers who are unable to make a large down payment. The credit score requirement for borrowers is much lower than conventional loan requirements. A 620 credit score is the norm that most FHA lenders want borrowers to have when applying for a loan. I've heard stories about some lenders even accepting a 580 credit score on a case-by-case basis with compensating factors. The down payment for an FHA mortgage is typically 3-3.5 percent down, which can be a gift from a family member. The FHA mortgage is a good way to get financing for a home if you do not have to have a high credit score.

For those of you who have served in any branch of the military, the VA loan is a great way to obtain a 100 percent financing for a new home. The VA loan is a guaranteed loan backed by the Department of Veterans Affairs, offering long-term financing for veterans and their surviving spouses. The underwriting criteria is similar to FHA, but a VA loan grants veterans 100 percent financing, while an FHA loan finances 96.5 percent of the purchase price. Both VA and FHA loans are guaranteed by the US Government, and approved lenders that offer these loans require in a 620 credit score. Government-insured mortgages also allow alternative credit to be considered when applying for a loan. Alternative credit is credit that a borrower may have that does not show on his/her credit report. Examples of alternative credit would be a cell phone, utility bills, furniture bills, etc.

The two best programs for traditional financing are FHA loans and (if you are a Veteran) VA loans. Most Americans are not veterans, but the following chapter will show you how to receive 100 percent financing even if you did not serve in the military.

Chapter 4.

<u>100 Percent Financing Through Investor Program</u>

I made a promise to keep this book short, direct, and to the point regarding 100 percent financing programs, so let me share the first program.

The first program that offers 100 percent financing is Home Partners of America. Home Partners of America has one of the best programs that I have seen in years. They don't just finance you 100 percent of the purchase price, they will actually buy the home for you. Yes, I know it sounds hard to believe. So, take a deep breath - inhale and exhale - and read the paragraph again. Now that you have absorbed and processed the program offered by Home Partners of America, take a deep breath once again and exhale because I'm about to share something else that is unheard of in traditional financing for real estate. The FICO score requirement is only a 525 credit score.

The way the program works is very simple for home buyers. Submit an application to Homepartnersofamerica.com to get pre-approved. Home Partners of America will check your credit, income, and background. The underwriting criteria is very simple. In most cases, if you can afford the home and you have been on your job for at least two years with no bankruptcies in the last two years, you will be approved. There are other factors that are considered and programs are subject to change, so feel free to contact them and ask any and all questions you have on your mind.

The only downside of buying a home through Home Partners of America is that this program only allows you to purchase single family homes. Residential two-to four-unit buildings are not allowed through Home Partners of America.

Buyers that use Home Partners of America are given a lease-with-option-to-buy agreement and the term offered is normally three to five years. In other words, you can lease up to three years and renew the lease for an additional two years.

The lease-with-option-to-buy agreement allows you to refinance the home based on the appraised value. There is not a time frame required before you can refinance. Under the lease-with-option-to-buy agreement you can refinance anytime you choose and pay off the lien holder, which in this case would be Home Partners of America.

Home Partners of America will charge you five percent of the purchase price as a fee for buying the home for you when you refinance the loan or pay them off the balance owed.

Using this method allows you to purchase your dream home and have an extended period of time to refinance or pay off the mortgage owed to Home Partners of America. If you have credit issues and need to bring your score up higher to refinance, you have at least three years, which is more than enough time.

Chapter 5.

<u>100 Percent Financing Through a Nonprofit Organization</u> (Free Information)

The next program that allows for 100 percent financing is through a nonprofit organization called Neighborhood Assistance Corporation of America (NACA).

NACA offers a very unique program that allows a buyer to receive 100 percent financing for their members with benefits that surpass 99 percent of traditional banks and lenders. NACA was originally formed to go after predatory lenders and has evolved to offer the best home mortgage that I have seen in my twenty-plus years of real estate.

One of the key points that sets NACA apart from the few lenders and banks that offer 100 percent financing is the simple fact that not only are buyers guaranteed a low interest rate but they are actually allowed to buy down their interest rate to zero percent. This is unheard of in the mortgage industry.

Yes, buying the interest rate down will require money when you purchase the home, but if you have the money saved and wanted to pay for a zero percent interest loan, you have that option at your fingertips.

Example "A"

Mortgage   300,000

Interest rate   3%

30 year mortgage   = $1,265 principle & interest

Below is the same example for buyers that have cash on hand to buy down the interest rate at the time of purchase.

Example "B"

Mortgage   300,000

Interest rate   0%

30 year mortgage   = $833 principle "No interest"

Over the course of a thirty-year mortgage, example "A" would pay $455,332 at a three percent interest rate.

Example "B" would pay no interest at all by buying the rate down to zero percent. And over the course of thirty years, the mortgage would simply cost the original purchase price of $300,000 plus the money spent to buy down the rate, thus saving the buyer over $125,000 over the course of the thirty-year mortgage.

The example above is just one of the many benefits that NACA offers to their members. Another benefit of becoming a member of NACA and buying a home through NACA is the buyer's choice of choosing between a single family home or a 2-4 unit building.

Smart buyers of real estate that use programs like the above-mentioned take advantage of first-time home ownership programs or 100 percent finance programs when buying a home. **Even if you are not a first-time homeowner, if you currently do not own any property in your name NACA will allow you to maximize your purchasing power by buying a 2-4 unit home at 100 percent financing or loan-to-value (LTV).**

Chapter 8 expounds on maximizing your purchasing power and getting the most out of 100 percent programs, first-time homeownership financing, and making money or living for free when you buy a two- to four-unit building. Please pay close attention to the details in Chapter 8 and recognize the easy way to save money and make money. One of the best benefits of becoming a member of NACA and getting financed through NACA is there is no FICO score requirement! Yes, let me write this again -- no FICO score requirements. NACA understands that credit scores do not tell the entire story of a person's life.

The major underwriting requirements for NACA are two years on the job or in the same line of work for two years, and a buyer's debt-to-income (DTI) ratio meeting the current guidelines. Most lenders want a buyer's DTI to be less than 45 percent of the buyer's monthly income. The DTI is a basic formula used by underwriters to see if a buyer can afford the home or two- to four-unit building they are looking to purchase.

Getting started with NACA requires a buyer to attend a workshop in which they expound on the process of buying a home through NACA and the benefits of becoming a member. NACA will assist you in obtaining financing in most if not all fifty states in the USA at 100 percent financing of the purchase price of a single family home or two- to four-unit building. Programs are subject to change, but with NACA, I believe they will only change for the better. For more information, visit the NACA website at naca.com.

Chapter 6.

<u>Land Contracts/Rent with an Option to Buy</u>

Land contracts are another easy way to purchase a home. Millions of consumers across the land are not familiar with land contracts. A land contract is a contract that allows you to purchase a home with, in most cases, a small down payment ($1,000 to $10,000) commonly referred to as "renting with an option to buy". You take possession of the property and you are placed on the title. You have a time frame of 12-24 months to pay off the balance, or whatever time frame agreed upon by both parties. The time frame of the contract and the amount of money placed down is dependent on what the seller and buyer agree upon.

What makes this program elite is the fact that in 95 percent of most cases, the buyer has bad credit and still gets a nice home. Remember that in real estate financing, the current rental history is the most important line of credit.

Example: A buyer purchases a home under a land contract for $250,000. The buyer places $10,000 down on the purchase of his or her new home. The land contract is made over a period of two years. The land contract or lease-with-option-to-buy agreement is accepted and the buyer moves into the property. The buyer takes possession of the property. The buyer's monthly payment is $1,500 including taxes and insurance.

The buyer decides to pay off the land contract early by refinancing the home after twelve months on the property. The appraised value of the property is $290,000. The buyer received an 85 percent loan-to-value (LTV) from the lender. The buyer could have received a higher loan amount, but he had a couple of credit cards that he did not pay on time within the last twelve months. The appraised value of $290,000 times 85 percent LTV equals a loan amount of $246,500. The buyer's payoff was $240,000. Fourteen hundred dollars was paid in closing costs and $5,100 went to the buyer.

The buyer received $5,100 of the original $10,000 used as a down payment back in their pockets. The buyer has released the seller of any interest they had in the property. The buyer now owns the property with a mortgage to the bank for $246,500.

Another smarter way, using the same principle of a land contract is wording the land contract as "rent with option to buy". When a buyer rents with an option to buy for a set term, usually one to two years, the renter or buyer is not obligated to purchase the home. The buyer or renter can simply leave the home when the rent-with-option-to-buy agreement has expired.

So, say the buyer tells the seller that he/she does not know if he/she will buy the home but would still like to have the option to buy in the agreement. The seller agrees and lets the buyer/renter rent for 24 months with an option-to-buy clause in the agreement. The seller asked the buyer/renter for one month's security deposit and the first month's rent since the buyer does not know if they will purchase the home at the end of the 24 months.

Both parties agree on the terms of the rent-with-option-to-buy lease agreement and the buyer pays the security deposit and first month's rent and moves into the property.

The buyer/renter decides to buy the home after two years and exercise the option to buy. The buyer/renter calls a mortgage company and applies for a mortgage. Instead of a traditional mortgage, the buyer/renter can refinance the home because he/she has lived in the home for over six months and is exercising his/her option to buy.

Now, if we use the example above and the buyer's purchase price is $250,00 and the home appraises for $290,000 at the time of the refinance. The lender refinances the buyer at a 90 percent LTV which comes out to $261,000 minus the payoff of $250,000, leaving the buyer with $11,000 available for closing cost and any upgrades to the home.

The difference between the two examples listed in this chapter is the first buyer only received an 85 percent LTV because of a couple of credit cards being delinquent and the second buyer received a 90 percent LTV. There is also a difference in the down payment or money initially spent to acquire the home using a land contract versus a rent-with-option-to-buy agreement.

In the land contract, the buyer placed $10,000 down at the time the agreement was executed and then moved into the home. In the second example, the buyer used a rent-with-option-to-buy agreement and only paid the first month's rent and a security deposit.

There is a clear distinction between the two examples listed above in this chapter. One buyer paid $10,000 down and the buyer in the last example paid his first month's rent and a security deposit that will be returned that came out to $3,000 dollars.

Who would you rather be in the examples above? The second buyer wins by $7,000 that was kept in his/her bank that was not used as a down payment. The security deposit was also returned to the second buyer when he/she refinanced the home to pay off the rent-with-option-to-buy contract, thus allowing the buyer to technically purchase the home receiving 100 percent financing. The second buyer also received cash back when the property was refinanced to pay off the current owner.

When refinancing a land contract or rent-with-option-to-buy agreement, most banks will offer one of two types of refinance loans: a "rate and term" refinance, which means the bank will only pay off the balance owed to the seller, or a "cash out refinance", meaning the balance owed to seller will be included in the loan and cash out to the owner for repairs, credit card bills, or simply cash.

Exercising knowledge obtained from experienced investors as you have just read can save you a lot of money. With land contracts and rent-with-option-to-buy agreements you can also have a certain amount or percentage of the monthly rent go toward the principle of the purchase price. This is why it is important to work with a seasoned professional to guide you through the home buying experience.

If you are in the market for a land contract or rent-with-option-to-buy agreement, contact your local Realtor. A lot of land contracts/rent-with-option-to-buy contracts are posted on the Multiple Listing Service commonly referred to as MLS. A "rent with an option to buy" contract or "land contract" are opportunities to own a home with little or no money down. Remember, the contract needs to state that you have the option to buy anytime throughout the term of this lease agreement.

Stay away from loan officers who tell you that they will have your contract backdated six months to one year so you can be financed for your home today. Be patient and wait out the six to twelve months to receive financing from a lender. It is illegal for you to backdate land contracts. Many loan officers have gotten into serious trouble for backdating contracts, so do not agree if ever asked to do it.

Chapter 7.

100 Percent Financing Using Hard Money

Although it's considered a hard money loan, Dohardmoney.com offers 100 percent financing on certain residential properties that can be purchased at a discount. A hard money loan is a higher interest loan for short-term use for the acquisition, purchase, rehab, or refinance of an investment property.

Laws on hard money loans vary from state to state and these loans are used by real estate investors for short-term use only. Typical terms and interest rates for hard money loans are normally from six months up to two years and the normal interest rates for hard money loans range from 12-21 percent.

Most hard money lenders charge between three to five percent of the loan that they give to their clients. For details, rates, and the entire break down of the 100 percent program offered by "Dohardmoney" simply visit "http://dohardmoney.com/"Dohardmoney.com.

Chapter 8.

<u>Getting Started</u>

Now that you are aware of the three ways that you can receive 100 percent financing on your new home, it's time for you to walk the path to home ownership. The first step in the process is to get pre-approved through one of the programs listed in previous chapters and decide what type of home you want to purchase.

As I mentioned in the previous chapter buying a two-four unit building through NACA is the best way to go. Remember Home Partners of America will only purchase single family homes for you.

Go to the NACA website and sign up for the next seminar in your area. Get familiar with NACA's website and feel free to reach out to them with any questions or concerns. After NACA's initial introduction seminar explaining their program, requirements, and guidelines you can schedule an appointment to bring in your income documents. A checklist will be provided to you outlining documentation needed to start the process of buying your home.

If you decided to buy a single family home as opposed to a two- to four-unit building, you can apply through NACA or Home Partners of America for 100 percent financing.

First things first - try your best to decide what you want to do based on your needs and desire. Weigh out your options and goals. If you have children, it's always best to think about their financial future and the cost associated with raising children today, along with the cost of education.

Once you have decided on a single family home or two-to four-unit building, the next step is to get pre-approved for your new home. Contact NACA or Home Partners of America and get pre-approved. In the pre-approval process, you will find out from the loan officer exactly how much you qualify for to purchase a home.

The pre-approval process is the most important process in purchasing a home. You can look at three homes a day for six months, but if you are not pre-approved, you are basically window shopping. Even if you are familiar with your credit score and you know that with a 720 credit score you meet the FICO score requirement that traditional banks require, you still have to consider your debt-to-income ratio and down payment for the home. The debt-to-income ratio is very important because it shows you, based on the bank's requirement, how much the bank is comfortable lending to a buyer. Most banks have a 45 percent back-end ratio. Meaning, your monthly bills cannot exceed 45 percent of your monthly income.

Once you are pre-approved for a set loan amount and decide what type of home you desire to purchase, your next step is to reach out to a Realtor to assist you in finding your new home. If you know investors that own properties and are actively seeking to sell their properties, feel free to reach out to them. A good site to find a variety of homes and two- to four-unit buildings is Zillow.com. Follow the prompts and type in the zip code where you desire to live. You can also find discounted deals there by looking for price reductions and analyzing the market time that a property has been on the market. In most cases, the longer a property has been on the market, the more motivated a seller will be to sell and discount a property.

Establishing or having good relationships with other professionals is a good factor to build a quality team to fulfill your dreams.

Chapter 9.

<u>Maximizing Your Purchasing Power</u>

Whether you are a first-time homeowner or if you have owned properties in the past but currently do not have any real estate in your name, the 100 percent program will still work for you, but it's important for you to maximize your purchase.

Once you purchase a home in your name, you will lose your status of a first-time homeowner. Pay close attention to this chapter because the following information is very important and can save you thousands of dollars while placing you in a excellent financial position to save money for future real estate properties.

The 100 percent program mentioned in previous chapters only applies to first-time homeowners or buyers that currently do not have properties in their name. After you have successfully purchased your first home, if you decide to buy income-producing property or any other real estate, the banks will view you as an investor. When banks underwrite real estate deals for investors, in most cases they require 20-25 percent of the purchase price as a down payment.

If you decided to buy a three-unit building for rental income after you have purchased a home in your name, below is an example of how most banks underwrite.

Example:

Purchase Price:	$300,000
Bank Loan Amount:	$240,000
Down Payment:	$60,000

As you notice in the example above, the bank would require $60,000 as a down payment which is twenty percent of the purchase price. That does not include closing cost for the transaction or hazard insurance. The bank will also want to see reserves in the bank or a savings account in your name. Reserves are money you have access to in the event of an emergency, unexpected repairs, etc. Traditional underwriters for banks like to see six months of the proposed new mortgage payment in a bank account.

Based off of the same example above, let's do a little math together. The bank offered you a six percent interest rate on the three-unit building that you desired to purchase, as opposed to a four percent interest rate because it's a multi-unit building with more risk involved for the bank. At a six percent interest rate, below is an example of a proposed new mortgage payment along with taxes, insurance, and average closing cost.

Principle & Interest Mortgage Payment:	$1,799
Taxes	$250
Insurance	$120
Total	**$2,169**

Now that you can visualize a proposed new mortgage payment on your new three-unit building, and you have a basic understanding of required reserves or what the bank typically expects as assets, let's do some more math and factor in closing cost.

The average closing cost at a purchase price of $300,000 would cost between seven and ten thousand dollars. Closing cost varies from city to city, and as a buyer, in most cases, you will receive a tax credit from the seller of prorated unpaid taxes that are not due at the time you purchase the home. But for this example, let's say the closing cost is $10,000 after any credits from the seller.

Adding up the closing cost, six months reserves, and down payment on the example above brings you to a total of $83,014.

Down Payment (20% of purchase price)	$60,000
Reserves ($2,169 X 6)	$13,014
Closing Cost (Estimate)	$10,000
Total	**$83,014**

Most people do not have $83,000 laying around to invest in real estate. Even if you decided to pull the money from your 401k, IRA, etc. to buy a multi-unit building to earn additional income, it still would not be a wise decision. Smart investors go out of their way to use the bank's money. The bank's money is insured, in most cases through mortgage insurance.

The example above is a clear indication of why it's better to buy a two- to four-unit building at 100 percent financing. Take advantage of your first-time homeowner option by maximizing your purchase with a two-to-four unit building using the 100 percent program. If you have owned properties before. You would still qualify as long as you do not have any properties in your name when you apply.

Even if you purchased the three-unit building through FHA under the first-time homebuyer program, you would still be required to put down three percent of the purchase price and pay closing cost. Three percent of a $300,000 home equals $9,000, and if you consider the average closing cost of, say, $7,000, you would be paying out of pocket around $16,000.

This is why I teach my clients to purchase two-to four-unit buildings first, and buy their dream home later. In the same example above, if you go through one of the 100 percent programs mentioned in this book and you purchased a three-unit building, you will not have to put $60,000 down on the building.

That saves you $60,000 in the beginning of your real estate career and if you buy a three-unit building that has tenants in the building, there is a good chance that you will be living for free and making money.

The average rent for a three-bedroom apartment in my city of Chicago is $1,000-$1,500 a month. So if you purchased a three-unit building and lived in one of the units while renting out the other two units for $1,300 a month, your gross income would be $2,600 a month.

Using the example above, your monthly payment would be $2,169. That payment is including principal, interest, taxes, and insurance (PITI) , leaving you with $431 per month in net rental income. But the most important attribute of owning a three-unit building in this example is that you are living for free. Yes, you are living rent free and you have tenants that are paying for your building and taxes from rental income.

Let's take the scenario a step further. From the example above, you are making $431 per month which equals $5,172 a year in net rental income, and you are living for free. If you decided to pay yourself $1,300 per month as if you were paying a landlord, you would save $15,600 a year. In a two year period, you would have saved $41,544.

Imagine the same scenario with a four-unit building earning $3,900 a month in rental income. Your savings over a three-year period would put you in a commanding position to purchase more real estate, build your net worth, and have a safety net for the future of your kids and yourself. Maximizing your purchasing power, as you can see from examples above, is a major step in building your financial future.

Chapter 10.

<u>Before You Become an Investor</u>

Take small steps toward your goals and establish a blueprint for investing that allows for you to have an emergency account or cash in the bank in case of an emergency. There are a lot of people that begin a career in real estate investing and get in over their head, or in the red, and wind up losing their properties. If you plan on building a portfolio of investment properties, you have to keep an emergency account and the proper insurance coverage for income-producing properties.

I can recall an investment property in Chicago that an Investor owned that had flood damage from heavy rains. The insurance company didn't pay the claim because the heavy rains caused the sewers to back up. The insurance company told the Investor that she didn't have backup insurance which is totally different from flood insurance.

The adjuster from the insurance company went on to say that this happens all the time and that whoever sold her the insurance policy should have explained that to her. This is a perfect example of the unexpected things that could happen that can put a new investor in the negative zone financially.

The repair cost for her basement unit wind up costing her additional $12,000. The sad part about this example is that the Investor had just spent around $17,000 renovating the entire basement unit of her building. This is why it's important to work with a seasoned professional that can explain and teach you the woes and simple principles to prevent major mistakes.

I can recall a fellow executive over 15 years ago who owned a two unit investment property. Everything was fine until he rented out his unit to some people who were referred by a friend. Since his friend referred the tenants to him, he didn't bother to do a credit check or background check on the tenants.

It wound up being his worst nightmare. Not only did he have to evict the tenants for not paying rent, but they also intentionally trashed the place. He called his insurance agent to file a claim and explained what happened. The insurance agent asked my associate, "Do you have vandalism insurance?" My friend and fellow executive responded, "No." The agent went on to explain to him that the insurance company cannot cover vandalism from a former tenant that was evicted because he didn't have vandalism coverage on his policy.

These are two examples of mistakes that new investors make. A lot of new investors wind up bankrupt or with properties in foreclosure because they did not know how insurance companies operate and the importance of having the proper coverage. Or, by being too nice and not following traditional background, employment, and credit checks. So, make sure you have the proper coverage on your home and investments properties. And most importantly, keep an emergency account or cash on hand just in case something out of the ordinary happens.

Chapter 11.

<u>Brokers/Realtors and Loan Officers</u>

Increase your business like never before by simply referring your clients that have credits issues or low credit scores to NACA, Home Partners of America, or by suggesting renting with an option to buy or a land contract. Revive those old deals and encourage clients to buy a copy of this book for their family and friends. Buyers with low credit scores have always been a challenge to get financed for a new home. Most Americans do not know about the programs listed in this book.

Just imagine the increase in your business and all the old clients that you can help purchase their dream home. I personally know several Realtors that are getting commission for helping landlords find tenants to rent homes and also receive commission when the home sells or is refinanced out of a land contract or rent-with-option-to-buy contracts. Make more money and enjoy the warm feeling that you get inside when you help a client fulfill their dream of becoming a first-time homeowner.

Chapter 12.

Purchasing Foreclosures or Distressed Properties

There are thousands of foreclosures and pre-foreclosures all across America. There are a lot of sites online that advertise the sale of foreclosure lists, which are public information. You don't have to purchase foreclosure lists from online vendors if you are pre-approved and working with a broker. The broker will be more than happy to look up foreclosures for you by zip code.

There are free websites such as Zillow.com and online auctions that sell bank-owned foreclosures. Below are a few sites that allow you to view foreclosures by simply entering the zip code or state.

Aution.com

Hubzu.com

XHome.com

http://foreclosures.bankofamerica.com/

http://www.hudforeclosed.com

When using these sites, make sure you work with a licensed Realtor if you do not have access to the MLS.

Zillow.com has links that allow you to look at homes sold in the subject area of the property that you are looking to purchase. Some people have said that the comparisons (or comps) at Zillow only show you a few homes in the area that sold. A licensed Realtor can confirm similar homes that have sold and you can also look at the tax records to see homes that sold recently that were not listed on the MLS.

Chapter 13.

<u>Asset-Based Lending</u>

Asset-based lending is a loan normally secured by collateral assets. The loan or line of credit can also be secured by inventory, accounts receivable, and/or other balance-sheet assets.

Asset-based lending is also known as "commercial finance" or "asset-based financing". This type of lending can come in handy if you find a good investment property and you don't have the 20-25 percent down payment to purchase the investment property.

Most of the lenders that offer asset-based lending do not require a credit check and simply lend off the value of the asset.

This is an alternative way to get financed for a short-term loan to achieve a certain goal. Most asset-based loans are considered hard money loans. However, there are several banks that offer fairly low interest rates. These lenders typically want to see a good credit score attached to your asset if they offer you a low interest rate on a short-term loan.

Signature Investments & Consulting Inc., the parent company of Financialsecretsrevealed.com, specializes in reaching and providing our clients with alternative lenders, investors, private money banks, and programs from lenders around the world. We also take pride in solving financial problems for our clients and have access to a variety of lenders that provide creative financing.

Funding and loan amounts vary from bank to bank and lenders normally lend between 50-75 percent loan-to-value.

Remember, in most cases asset-based loans from the lenders that we network with do not require good credit, financial statements, or tax returns. Loans are approved and funded strictly off the value of the asset. Below is a list of approved assets from a sound lender to whom we refer our clients for asset-based loans.

Qualifying Assets:

Precious Metals	Aircraft
Gemstones	Diamonds
New Luxury Cars	Boats

Oil	Jewelry
Yachts	Medical Equipment
Used luxury Cars	RV's, Motorcycles

Remember, asset-based lending is primarily used to achieve a short-term goal. It is simply another method to raise capital short-term.

Chapter 14.

Principles to Success and Wealth

Loyalty produces royalty. There are so many people
that belittle, disrespect, and wrongly treat good people
who have helped them along the way. These people
burn bridges and wonder why life is hard for them. In
the Bible, Jesus healed ten people of leprosy disease
and only one of them came back to tell him, "Thank
you." (Luke 17:11-19 KJV) I've seen this type of behavior
in business and it literally offends good people and
causes people to stray away from the individual that
behaves that way.

Most wealthy people keep an inner circle of people that
they respect, love, and trust. People in the inner circle
of trust have proven their loyalty and have fringe
benefits for being loyal. Successful men don't have a
problem sharing their money and new ideas with loyal
people. Money can come and go but favor for loyal
people lasts a lifetime. I cannot tell you how many times
I've been given financial secrets over the years by
wealthy people just for being loyal. So, always be loyal
and watch the favor of God and good people will come
your way.

Treat people like you want to be treated. When I was a little boy growing up, my mother often told me this saying. And, not only did I apply it in day-to-day life, but I also applied this principle in business. The principle sounds simple or elementary to some people but those are usually the people that don't apply it. Then, they wonder why their business is falling. Treating clients, tenants, or consumers well will increase your business and give you a great reputation.

Kings & queens are established in life based on their ability to solve problems. People are often promoted into jobs based on their ability to solve problems. Millionaires are created, in a lot of cases, by solving a problem. Providing a place for a family to rent in a good neighborhood is solving a problem.

Loan officers refinancing a client's home from a six percent interest rate to a three percent interest rate is solving a problem and saving consumers money. I complained last year about how much money I spent a month on gas riding around all day looking at different real estate properties. I looked in the mirror and quickly corrected myself. I drove to a Toyota dealer and purchased a hybrid that gets 52 miles per gallon instead of the ten to twelve miles a gallon I was getting in my so-called luxury vehicle.

Whether you purchase a home for your kids or become a huge investor, you can always make money by solving someone's problems.

Self-discipline is a major key to unlocking your doors to success. Having the discipline to save your money and be a good steward of your credit can take you to very high places in life. Successful business owners know first-hand how many hours they had to work to make their business successful.

Oftentimes, people look at the end results of a successful business person but never saw the hard work, long hours, financial sacrifice, and discipline the business owner had to apply. There's a saying that a lot of business owners like to say when asked about their struggle starting and maintaining a business -- and that saying is, "Blood, sweat, and tears." It sounds harsh, but the rewards of self-discipline and focus bring a better quality of life. They bring a bigger and better place to stay, and most importantly, financial freedom for your family.

Humility is a key that wise people exercise daily. Be humble. Attitude determines altitude. Whether you are getting started, a broker, or a seasoned investor making a six-to eight-figure annually, always stay humble. "And whosoever shall exalt himself shall be abased; and he that shall humble himself shall be exalted" (Matthew 23:12 KJV). Being humble will put you in the presence of strong, good people. No one likes a jackass, or a pompous person always bragging about what they have and how much they have accomplished. People that walk in pride are selfish, self-centered, and greedy. Humble people are the exact opposite. They always look to give and share, and they are driven by purpose. So, always exercise humility because not only will you have the favor of God, but you will also have the favor of good people.

Stay away from negative people because they will always try to prolong your vision or blessing and bring you down. Haters and negative people will always say, "You can't do this," or, "You shouldn't do that," when it comes to your dreams and business ideas. The negative energy they produce daily slowly pulls on your strength and positive energy. So, steer clear of the vision-killers and stay humble because there is a very good chance they will ask you for advice or a job in the future.

Knowledge is power. The more you know, the higher you can go in life. A wise man once told me that a king knows a little bit about everything. Always strive for perfection and to be a good listener regardless of whether you are interested in what a person is saying to you or not. Hear a person out when they are sharing information because you never know what you might need in the future. Programs constantly change and new programs are constantly being written. Banking laws change and bright minds create new and innovative inventions, programs, and ideas annually.

The more you listen, the more you learn. If you are around a so-called investor or fellow professional and you can never get a word in a conversation, that is a sign to go another direction. Never partner with or put a person on your team that thinks they know everything. That negative spirit is like mold and will slowly spread to others. Have the knowledge and understanding to love some people from a distance.

Build a team of like-minded competent professionals. No matter how gifted you are, there is no such thing as a one-man army. Eagles do not fly with chickens. Eagles soar high in the sky and can see miles away. Chickens are always looking down and cannot fly as high as eagles. A good team will take you to high places and share knowledge, thus making the team strong.

Put God first in your business ideas and plans. The Bible says to "Trust in the Lord with all your heart and lean not into your own understanding. In all your ways acknowledge him and he shall direct your path" (Proverbs 3:5-6 KJV). This scripture does not just apply to your spiritual walk with God, but it applies to every area and concern of your life.

There is nothing like having the favor of God in your business. There is safety in numbers or a board of directors when it comes to business. However, it is a beautiful thing when you can consult The King of

Kings regarding your business. There is nothing like having an invisible cell phone to Heaven that allows you to get on your knees and converse with "The Lord of Host" speaking directly to Heaven. When you put God first and treat people like you want to be treated, you don't have to worry about referrals. People will always flock to individuals that have a good aura.

Chapter 15.

<u>Dream Big, Live Large</u>

Don't ever stop dreaming and using your imagination to fulfill your dreams. I've seen so many people over the years give up on their dreams and settle for less - living paycheck to paycheck, just as the system designed for the majority of Americans.

Emergencies happen in life, and not having money when a problem occurs can be a catastrophe. Having the discipline to apply the basic principles in this book for an investment property is big start in the process of becoming financially independent. Imagine receiving over $10,000 a month in rental income for the rest of your life from just a few three-to-four-unit buildings, in addition to your nine-to-five job that you decided to keep until you are a millionaire. It sounds far off to some, but you have investors making three million a month in rental income that started small with two-to four-units and worked their way up to seven figures a month.

People often say that "money does not bring happiness". Often people use that common saying as an excuse to give up on their dreams. But, if you ask those same people if they would like to live in a bigger house, send their kids to a private school, or take more vacations, their answer changes.

Let's face the facts. Money cannot bring you happiness, but it can bring you a better class of living. You can give more to your church or favorite charity, feed the homeless, buy fatherless children clothes and school supplies, and most importantly show some love, not just in words but deeds.

If a person is happy with a two bedroom apartment that's fine. I know millionaires that live in apartments. The point being made is to pursue your happiness in life and make money to be a blessing to someone else. In this world money is right next to oxygen so make as much as you can and take good care of the people you love.

The sky is the limit. Fulfill your dreams. Dream big, live large!

www.ingramcontent.com/pod-product-compliance
Lightning Source LLC
Chambersburg PA
CBHW020318220326
41598CB00017BA/1597

* 9 7 8 0 9 7 1 6 1 7 9 1 9 *